£3

DÜRER 'S HARE

Dürer's Hare

Anna Wigley

Gomer

First Impression – 2005

ISBN 1 84323 498 X

© Anna Wigley

This book is published with the financial support of the Welsh Books Council.

Printed in Wales at
Gomer Press, Llandysul, Ceredigion SA44 4JL

CONTENTS

ACKNOWLEDGEMENTS

Some of these poems first appeared in the following magazines: *BBC Wildlife Magazine, Borderlines, New Welsh Review, Planet, Poetry Review, Poetry Wales, Yellow Crane.*

The Jackdaw in the Wind

Suddenly he blew in and was beside us:
tattered ghost of the crag,
with bent feet and wings braced
against the slamming door of wind.

For many seconds he hovered there,
not quite outfacing the violent air,
not letting it take him either.

If he pitted his flexible ounces
against the bouldering barrage
it was not in some grim struggle
but as a game that tested all he was –

all his delicacy and daring.
Behind him the gaunt hill
flattened its grasses, the granite winced.
But the jackdaw danced

in the sky without moving,
staring out the void
with his lightless eye;
a tremor in the blast, treading nothing.

Llanthony Abbey

A kite chose the spot:
wheeling above the clefts
where mountains meet,

a bird's vision pictured
stone arches, lightly laced.
A painter of road

tagged this abbey to the world,
while it floated far out
in the green sea of hills.

Near as the monks could get
to Eden, it neighboured
buzzards' nests,

battered statues of oaks.
Now horses tilt their heads
in its shadow, the hall

is sown with violets.
A warm wind follows us
through blown windows,

and martins stitch and stitch
the gaping frames
with invisible thread.

Architects of sun
and shade, of leaf
and stone and cloud,

laid these ancient walls;
putting one church
inside another,

so the monks,
when they looked up,
might see in a slope of bracken

or a winter tree's
stark epigram,
fragments of holy writ.

Dürer's Hare

Still trembling, after five hundred years.
Still with the smell of grass
and the blot of summer rain
on her long, thorn-tipped paws.

Look how thick the fur is,
and how each thistledown hair
catches the light
that glistens even in shadow
from the trimmed plush of the ears.

How did he keep her still?
She was crouched there long enough
for him to trace the fragile hips
and ribs beneath the mink,

to feel the pale edges
of the belly-pouch,
the sprung triggers of the flanks.
The nose shimmers
where the short hairs grow in a rosette.
Go on, touch it.

For she's only here for a moment,
Dürer's hare;
the frame can barely hold her.
Her shadow is a shifting thing,
slippery as a raincloud in wind,
and even as you look,
twitches to be gone.

Wings

What are these
wings
you have brought me

branching at night
from my thin
shoulders

like two pale birds
restlessly
trying their feathers;

in the black
silence
they blossom

and itch
as I turn, adjust
to their weight

already lifting me
from my nest
of dead twigs,

pulling the soft
half-reluctant
flesh

upwards with
the eagle-fierce
levers of love.

Days

The days lie idle in their wrappings
until you come to undo them.
Colours from a busy sky
fill my room and fade
for lack of attention.

The weather of your eyes
is all the change I gauge
with my wands of bronze;

the stars exist to listen
to your laughter down my spine
and the one-word poem of your name.

The Seabed

I found your face on the seabed.
It was drowned in the undulating corals
and the silent bliss of fish
silvering through shadows.

I created your brow
with the gentle fever of my fingers.
It was the width of a crab,
new-made and a miracle.

You were there with me
with your toes in the silken silt
and your belly pale as a flounder,
your dreams lightly rippling

and every star pulled down,
every fathom of the copulating void
brought to you through the dark
currents of my sea-hands.

Far and Close

Five times I ran to you in the night.
Across the swarming hills of sleep
I saw the golden window of your face
shining in the valley's cleft.

I saw the gables of your arms,
the warm hearth of your breast.
Two birds flew from your eyes
to perch on my hands.

All the while you were lying quite still
in the distant house of your dreams.
It was the only way I could reach you,
running through those high black hills.

After Christmas

It leans against the wall, waiting,
the present I bought for you, waiting.

I wrapped it in the last red leaf
of my heart, the last leaf

I caught as it was falling.
It's bright as hope, the wrapping,

but now the paper's fading;
with every day it's fading.

January

The days go by like exhausted ghosts.
At dawn, in their grubby shifts
they trail down the blackened grates
of streets, and their faces glisten
with the no-colour pearl of ham bones.
What were we woken for?
Not for this scene of wet ashes
where no light can take hold and bud,
and granite skies bear down
on a single grassblade, a scattering of birds.

Brownbird

Brownbird
with soft sienna breast

and such calm feathers
– so closely fitted;

you landed in my path,
your cinnamon-coloured head

held high and alert,
your throat of fawn,

wings of mink folded;
and hopped three steps,

listened for a worm,
then pulled it.

Such a watercolour
of sorrel and hazelnut;

such a full finish
to your heavy curves;

you made your famous mate
seem like the false prince

dressed in borrowed robes,
while you, the true blueblood,

lived in the wood
waiting to be discovered.

Marigolds

From their bindings they unravel
like dusky lettuces.

Bitter tang of earth
musks their breath,
and dark crumbs reach
to their shoulders.

Petal after scorched petal
eats the heat
until they have it all.

At dusk the garden hearth
will be starred with their cinders.

Summer Rain

The window smears
with its small fingers

the Gaugin pinks
of the geranium.

The fuchsia deepens
by a shade

and the honeysuckle shatters
another phial of perfume.

An hour ago
it was mid-July,

the bees were dipping
with their orange thighs

and leaves made dark
handprints of shadow.

An hour from now
the rain will be

a spangle on warm grass,
surprisingly wet.

Cathays Cemetery

Here the dead are long dead.
Stone angels ten feet high
have raised their wings for a hundred years
or more, and do not tire,

unabashed by wind and wars.
Lichen spreads its stain
over the period names:
over Violet, Myrtle and Edward.

It belongs now to the birds.
The graves are sturdy branches
where magpies balance their robes
of blue satin, and crows

lift heavy flight into the gloom.
A bramble's iron skein
lays snares in the grass; cobwebs glisten
after rain. And no one listens

but the dead and their familiars,
the birds guarding their beds
with stately poses, to the trees
singing elegies in the wind.

August Midnight, Lilstock

Stars brailled the black;
a blind man's
new-broached book.

So felted was the dark
it hung on us in folds
of powdered cloth,

wooing a feathery call
from the owl's throat. Lie down, look up

you said, sprawling
in drunken awe
on the night's cliff-edge

under distances
that burst our gauges'
shuddering glass.

An electric moon
chalked shadows by your head
as you took another swig

of the sweet, benumbing fathoms
that swayed you out
beyond the lee of the hedge

and the rustling cowshed,
into the stilled gavotte
of bear and plough.

Again the owl hooted,
velvety as cow's breath
in the downy darkness.

I should have joined you there
on the ghostly tarmac
and cast my gaze afloat

like yours, on the open sea
of the star-speckled night,
and not called you back;

should have drunk long
of the indigo deeps
and the owl-opening moon

until the frozen swirl
of stars drew us into sleep
– a sleep into which we would fall

without effort, like gulls
hypnotized by thermals
and the racing of tiny waves.

Lynton

is an eagle's nest pinnacled
on purple cliffs.
The path totters up
ladder-steep
through pine-shadow
and the barren cries of gulls.
Behind, the sea falls
and shrinks to its own echo.

Houses and gravestones strain
against toppling, braced
to stop the drunken swoon
into nothing.
One black velvet evening

we climb higher still
to the uppermost tiers
through moon-whited lanes
to a terrace with a hand rail.

Level with the stars
we look down on a hundred castles
windowed with gold.
Beyond, the shawling ocean
and the ogre-shouldered hills.

Porlock

That was the day we heard the owl
– do you remember?
The sound of water
followed us all through the hours
in the wood of young oaks
with its loose floor of pebbles
as we wove and climbed,
an ache in our thighs,
while leaf shade kept
our bent heads cool.
Not until we'd left the village road
far behind, dropping the tether,
did we hear the owl's cry:
the voice of an unhappy ghost
loosing his lonely note
unanswered on the empty air.

Emily Brontë

His hawthorn heart
beat in hers;
not twisted by the winds, merely –
but by some kink in the seed
that bent the wood.
She might have carved a silhouette
of herself against a skyline at dusk –
a solitary, ancient hieroglyph.
And clutched the earth with feet
like tendrils of rock;
celandines round the roots,
plovers calling from the branches.

Penzance

Everything slopes down to the sea.
Streets pour themselves
over ledges and the sides of hills.
Nothing stops

till it reaches the one destination.
The high street's a rock
that rears and humps
over wreaths of foam.

In every alley, in every house,
you can hear him,
the excluded guest

– the black sheep of Penzance,
the violent unruly one
cut out of the patriarch's will,
come back for his inheritance.

Snail

Slender-horned traveller
of the lawn's rainforests;

thoughtful scholar
of the luscious glade;

questing across prairies
for green in ever-paler shades.

The grail of the tender shoot
awaits you in fields of clay;

and the marigold buds
like saffron-scented cakes.

So venture out now
in the minor keys of rain,

charting, with your lucent frills,
the world's weave and grain.

Scale cliffs of moist walls
on the scent of cellulose;

then feel your way back
to the rainwashed path.

And when night comes, gorge
on the blazing palette

of petunias, on purples
and electric pinks,

like an aesthete
with exotic tastes.

Your slowness is a gift
sages suffer to acquire.

Let your two senses tour you
through green basilicas,

through the marzipan walls
of wet cathedral choirs.

Dyffryn

Summer

The festival of leaves . . .
green on green
champagne overspill
on the dumbstruck lawns.

Hushed discoveries
in the small, unlocked rooms:
creepered arches,
a grove of scented pines,

and falling on sun-warmed stone
a wistaria's exuberance
of purple spiralling.
Were they waiting for us,

these parcels of Eden?
They seem so absorbed and content
in their own flowering,

like the coppery fish in pools
suspended in dreams
or twisting through shadows.

The lime tree's galleon
sways at the far end;
we pass and it salutes us
with a ruffle of sails.

Winter

A granite light
on gaunt walls; an indestructible
ivy rope the one survivor
of an epidemic of frost.

Faggots of trees
sharp as the air's breath
that is always almost
congealing to crystal.

Two crows flapping
ragged silhouettes
from lawn to chimney pot.
No fish in the lily pond,
no flesh on the wistaria bones,
no petal remaining
in the rose garden;

but a desolation of stalks
and coils of thorn toughening
under a bloom of ice.

Each garden now
is a little mausoleum
of thin, dry remains.
A burial plot
with no epitaph, save

a memory of red
in the haw clusters.

Alleys

The walls are crazed
with sun and sparrows.

The buddleia's spirals
broach their hives:

for a flutter of wings
today they are anybody's.

Light falls loose
on loose stones

crumbled in the alley;
the only shadows left

hide in the rubbery ivy's
mad dreadlocks. Cats

are stationed on every corner
ready to be rolled:

touch one with your finger,
watch it fall open.

Coal Tit

From the back window
a slice of October morning
drying like a rinsed glass.

From the hydrangea hedge
small skitters and scutterings:
minnows breaking a surface.

Then suddenly, there,
where a swag of yellow berries
hangs thick by the gate,

a blur of flight
and a coal tit in his tribal paints
sways on a toothpick twig.

The seedsock is a banquet on a hook.
He scatters it. Then he rests:
a jewel in the wet light.

Above, in a glitter of birch leaves,
more birds tip the water-jugs
of their song; it splashes down

and hearing it, the coal tit
spins off, his small sharp mass
dissolving in a flurry of wing-dust.

White-Bearded Lizard

You passed him to me; and in my hand
I held a small pale dragon.

I was his rock for the moment:
on stumpy legs he climbed
the living stone of my palm.
He was dry as powdery sand,
cool as a purse of calf-skin.

Into that winter room
he brought a whiff of legends,
the ache of a desert sun.

How absolutely still he was –
locked with the patience of a mountain
into his long meditation.
His eyes, two drops of bronze,
never moved from their inward attention.

Only his softly spined chin
lifted at the stroke of my finger
with the old familiar pleasure,
spinning between us a moment's bridge
of bright, fine, slipping sand.

Sea Lions

If water had a shape it would be theirs:
a seamless, tapering pod
pinched at one end to a paddle,
at the other to a puppy's head.

Nothing impedes their flow
through blue shadows, or fails
to lift them like ponderous balloons
above the soft sea-fields.

Propelled on half-finished wings
through elastic water,
they push their long-prowed noses
upwards through glassy silence.

A mournfulness is their element;
a wistfulness for a world
more silent still, without haste,
where even the seabed floats
on fin-clumps of grass.

Their lashless eyes seem fixed
on some inward meditation or loss.
They dance a majestic lament, as if
they remembered a life on the land
– but dimly, as in a dream,
and with a mild regret.

Crab

made of fired clay
and tiny pebbles,

sunk in his dusty bed
of shale and shingle;

scuttles from his hide
when the rock is rolled,

all trundling legs
and nut-brown shell;

sends up a puff of silt
and is lost from sight,

his edges melted;
then a scrabble,

and his red stones
are pincers;

he's burying
his soft nugget

in a dune of grit,
hiding in the smoke

of sand and mud
his ounce of strangeness.

Shells

I came on another today –
one of those chapels
standing like ruined mills
closed on their silence,
nursing the ghosts
that cling to their pews.

You can see them often
in mining towns
and at ends of roads
remaindered in the city,
their faces vacant,
their figures tall and shabby.

They loom like aged parents
cut adrift by decay,
the mocked shadows
of their lost, solid selves;

buildings that once
threw a bridge to heaven
and now fling their arches
into nothing

like the weed-riddled stones
of viaducts, that were
the tramlines of an empire
but point the way
now, to empty air.

Cat

still warm on hot tarmac
in his last sleep

under sun that is drying
the coin of blood

and stroking up the shine
on the coat of ash and honeywood.

His paws, four sooty flowers
just plucked, lie limp;

his tail a boa
of palest fawn

is strewn in a kink,
a question;

and every mark remains,
each tiny perfection

– the shadow at the ear-tips,
nostrils etched in ink –

the craftsmanship
of aeons

here among blown papers,
the indifference of cars;

swirling smuts
his only benediction.

Pygmalion

That summer, she wanted
not quite to disappear
but to rise clear of her flesh
as if from a block of marble

daily chipping at the fat
with her new, lethal will

and seeing first a scapula
then a wrist
grow into their fragile shapes

until she had created a girl
like Degas's little dancer –
with the same daisy-stalk legs
and bird-wing shoulders.

Then when she had lifted this creature
from her trap
she fell in love with her,
turning, every hour, to the mirror

where her mackerel-slender calves
flashed, and her hip bones were sharp
as the hollowed shell of a crab.

She kept her on lettuce and water
in a high stone tower –
nobody could reach her.

And she learned the price of art:
the loneliness, the hunger –

but it was worth it;
for her feet hardly grazed the ground
anymore. She knew the feather's
love-affair with air,
the moth's infatuation with fire.

Dinner

To Liz

You arrive with the dusk,
handing me the shadows
with your light coat.

I hang them both
in the lamplit lobby
of slumped shoulders.

At the table's end
three candlesticks float
flame from their fingers

and glasses tilt fire
in their broad bowls.

You sit where the flame
spins webs of copper
from your hair,

pours gold on your shoulders.
It is summer
and this is our hundredth dinner;

the years crowd the dark
spaces at our elbows,

the guttering candles
like our laughter
flaring up at odd moments.

Lamby Way

Marsh-tang and sea-tang
flavour the air strong

and a hundred yards in
to this no-man's land

you lift your arm, saying
'kestrel – there, hovering!'

and a rag flutters
the air, then is pulled

like a pierced kite
to the wind-bent grass.

Moorhens scud
the scum of algae

in the unflowing river,
threading the reeds,

the spears of bullrushes
and horse-high grasses

that stoop their manes
in the bullying breeze.

A solitary swan
revolves on her reflection,

carrying the vessel
of her treble clef.

Beyond her the heath-grass
stiff as a sailor's beard

crests the mud's mosaic
of glinting silt

where rubbery swags
of weed are strewn

like lost hairpieces
of mermaids, and bird skulls

lie scattered,
thin as blown eggs.

Now there is nowhere else,
horizons of cold water

are the only destination.
On the road back you point

to a tattered field of oaks
where three herons are lifting

their heavy sails,
dragging the ropes of their feet

clear of anchor,
hauling themselves upwards

to the seaborne currents
where they drift like skinny angels.

The Ward

The nurses rustle their wings of starch.
They have flesh enough for all of us
and the tremorless eyes of seasoned gods.

Each bed awaits its news.
Blinks slowly on its own rescue
and confesses this is home at last.

Irises have the skins of new birds' mouths
and oranges blaze like totems
among the homely plumbing of drips,

the dragon names of drugs.
By evening limbs are febrile in their sheets,
the sighs escape like petals

from a falling flower.
Each bed is islanded in lamplight
where a child waits for a kiss,

a careful pressing of the wrist,
the last communion wafer.
Sleep will not pull its hood over

though the brilliant corridor
goes now on softer soles
and is feathered with mothers' gossip.

The Heart's Crumb

The human heart
planted in its crumb of soil
sends out ingenious tendrils,
wrings oceans
from a single moisture drop,
clutches the particle of earth
till it becomes a field.

Letter from my Father

A page slips from the bundle
like a pressed flower.
A note written on scrap paper.

No need to read the words.
His hand strikes out
cancelling the years.

These Viking letters
show no decline,
no spidery hesitation.

Instead they breast the page
like the prow of a long ship
to all four corners.

The Moon at 3 a.m.

I was woken by the moon
staring at me like a summoner
waiting for an answer.

I do not know what answer
the moon waited for.
But my soul shrank like a fox

caught in the beam of a torch
as it slinks from the henhouse.
Oh dreadful time

to wake, in the smallest hour,
in the moon's Jehovah gaze,

my little room chased
beyond hiding, my soul
with the steel on its fur.

The Sea Room

The room they gave us
was made of sellotape and sawdust.

Tilting towards the street, it creaked
with the ghostly feet of the guests above
that restlessly walked the plank
from dawn onwards.

Our bed was a slab of rock
with a wafer of wool.
Wringing a pinch of comfort
from fleshless pillows
we slept thinly, our dreams policed

by overworked chambermaids
waiting with their pails of bleach
and the breakfast chef
up since four, dripping over the last
two leathery chipolatas.

But the room they gave us
was a cabin on a great ship:
each night we were rocked
from our moorings by a black forest;

each morning we woke
to the glory-song
of blue water, miles of it
cramming our walls with light.

The Blue Skirt

Today you bought a blue skirt,
wandering small among the shop rails
that after twelve sequestered months
were exotic as Tibet.

Feel it, you said,
holding up the sheeny petal of the cloth,
then letting it float.

It was no ordinary blue,
and as you moved
it also moved through many hues,
as if the blue of forty fields

where speedwell and forget-me-not
grow thick as thistles,
was cropped and threaded in its folds.
You swung it like a gorgeous girl

and later wore it full and loose
with silk and downy wool.
Under it, your burning hip
half-eaten, hardly showed.

Cooling

Over the houses the gulls
hump their wings and cruise
the new, rougher waves.

The sycamore leaves
are shingle, dragged under
the irregular breakers.

Laurels are skittish again
in the hedges; cats
have their fur parted

by the cold breath,
and the already-blown roses
are loosened by another stitch.

All down the streets
the currents funnel and twist
the wicks of shrubs,

shudder privet,
run quick shadows
across lawns

like clouds over water.
The cats freeze then scuttle,
birds take their chance

on a shuttle of breeze.
Upstairs a window rattles,
a door gets suddenly furious.

A Crescent Winter

A crescent winter
hangs, a glass sliver,

in this October's
blue fire

at six
when the bells toll clear
as the pulse of a river

and leaves of the sun
flake crinkled copper,

laughing up kerbs,
embroidering mortar,

feathering sills
where cats paint themselves;

and it whets the edges
of the moon,
the sky-cliffs

clean as cathedrals
etched

against fish-cold
rinsed heaven;

shaves its woodcut
in the early shadows.

November Trees

The lamps are going out one by one.
The wind is breathing on them.
A few rags of light drift to the ground and die.
A swarm of starlings wet as the rain
is excited by the blue sun.
Cars sigh through the gutter tides.
The trees are striding out to meet the northern waters
with no protection, their thighs like iron.

The Comb

My blue comb fell out onto the grass
and lay there like a traitor's kiss.
Both of us stopped and stared at it.
Soft rain began to fall, the graves
were leaning their white-rusted heads,
and in the deep grass my blue comb glowed.
I want to look nice for you, it said.

Home

You are the fire that comes to warm me.
Within your arms the cold dissolves;
the lost hope finds it was not lost.
Though you burn, you do not burn me.
Around my bones you wrap and weave
new flesh and skin, new sleeves
that cover me when you're gone.
See, you have sheathed me top to toe,
sewn me into this coat until
I am free to move every limb.

Litter

Something stirs
in leaf litter

under the roof
of brown scales

between the husks
scattered like butts

of spent cigars
a movement

in the fertile dark
a slither

eyeless
a hand of legs

touching forwards
under shelter

in a waste
of fallen timbers

crumbled mortar
the dark tangle

of old wrappings
wet grass

life stirs
grows succulent

on steaks of earth
larders of rot

and brings the birds
the feather-bright

mess-praising
winter birds.

Snow Scenes after Sisley

I

This is not the land it was.
The light and the elements are altered.

If it is not quite day
neither is it night, though moon
has mingled with sun
and trapped these faggots
of purple trees in its pool.

There are no shadows –
unless you call a blue glaze
trembling beside a wall, or the hump
of amethyst next to a trunk,
shadows.

But there is gloom:
buried in the white,
in the pale prismatic cloth,
the rose and hyacinth crystal.

It gathers in the still, distant trees
that stand like a painted backdrop.
It thickens the violet hills.

Footsteps in the lane will hack
half-hollowed caves of blue.

II

It is the woollen sky
— without window or cloud
or any variation,
humming heavy
on the neck of fields,
its boulders of smoke
massed as far as eye can follow;
its slate fog
having swallowed the other sky,
its clear-eyed brother —

it is this sky
that makes possible these streets
of tender twilight;

unearthly reflections
from the moulded snow;
whiteness in the shadows under walls,
and the rosy haze of grey
binding the distant field.

Even at noon the far trees
shimmer on the hills, and dissolve
beyond the white flag
of a church roof.

III

A black bird flaps free
of the silence; alights

on the snow-furred top of a tree
like Noah's dove –

new creature, in a new universe.

IV

The light is going now –
but the snow remains.
Trees and houses once more
change colour.
Strange, polar lights
play on the immaculate roofs
and travel through the streets.
White ground rises up
more real than anything
under our creaking feet –
already our deep tracks
in the sporous air
are hardening to ice.

Hill

Winter has stripped it
like a blanched nut;

now it rises clear
of flower and leaf
in stony stillness.

The air is pained
with white; ice

ribs in glass
the hawthorn bark.

Crooked limbs,
crabbed claws of twigs;

shock of frost
on the pebble earth.

On the Beacons

Under a spell
the mountain stream hung

its ladder of white sticks
badly joined. Steps

of plate glass,
fringes of flowing stone

were laced with ligaments
of ice; and wedding veils

hung from high shelves,
yards of tulle bundled

in cavities,
rock to the touch.

Under a window of hard water
a green weed spread forever.

At what moment
had movement set

into stillness:
how had the snake of water

failed to slip its cord
past enchantment?

Under the bubbled eye
of an ice pavement

something now moved in secret
– an asp of mercury

kept the old path open;
kept faith with the fern

in its womb of earth,
flashed to the cold sun.

Southerndown

A cliff hunches
against the edge of nothing.
Bulky shoulders
raised against wind
and extinction.
A hibernating bear,
its green-tufted fur
braving the terrible spaces,
the feral air;

crouched on the ledge of itself,
but leaning out
like Adam's hand
into silent gardens of stars.

Winter Beeches

A smoke-blue January dusk.
Membrane of frost on stone
and hedge-berries glowing
from their shadows' nest.

A line of beech trees
has cast its tangled mesh
against the sky; and now
the branches vault and clot

like ruined churches.
Sharp and dark they stand
in the soft flame of twilight,
this their hour

of intricate embroidery,
black thorns stitched
to vanishing point
on the cusp of night.

Garth

A December sun's
milky flame
running

to red rivers
lapping black
corals of trees

gathers the valley
in nets
of red shadow

lighting one last
star
in the gorse

bringing up
the night in velvet

winds
from the owl's throat.

February 8th

Today, the first daffodil.
Not quite unwrapped
but risking its tender silks
on the new brash light
like a half-opened baby's fist.

Courage in silence.
Noiseless slow birth.
The dead wrappings shed
in a caul, still hanging.

A hint of wetness
in the half-asleep head,
a vulnerable moment

before crispness,
before the rearing standard
is stiffened and raised,

stuck brave
and absolutely straight
in its inch of earth.

THE Bird
Hospital
Anna Wigley

The Bird Hospital is Anna Wigley's first collection of poetry.
Critically acclaimed, it focuses on the intricacies of the
natural world and the startling emotional revelations of
intimate moments.

ISBN 1 84323 068 2

£6.95

Anna Wigley's *Footprints* is a collection of short stories, each tale
in turn sketching the fleeting impression of a particular place,
scene or occasion. The moods vary from story to story: the
breezy and the melancholy keep company with the evocative
and exuberant. The schoolgirls on the weekend bus rub
shoulders with the pompous professor; likewise the crooked
librarian and the foundling kitten . . .
In its sympathetic observation of everyday life and in its poetic
precision of language, *Footprints* is a collection that is here to stay.

ISBN 1 84323 277 4

£6.99